The Cloudy Day

The Cloudy Day

Story and Pictures by J.H. Stroschin

REGNERY/GATEWAY, INC.
South Bend, Indiana

Library of Congress Catalog Card Number: 79-65792
International Standard Book Number: 0-89526-099-9

to my favorite
cloud watchers—
Laura, Brian, Evan,
Elizabeth and Paul
—and especially Henry

As Laura and Brian went outside to play
they knew something special would happen that day.

Their eyes searched the sky—there was so much to see above the old fence, near the gnarled oak tree.

Huge clouds, pushed by wind,
how they moved and then changed

billowing, blowing, and building—how strange!

See there! a plump puppy who sat near his dish

turned into a dragon making a wish.

And there a fine lion with a powerful yawn

became all at once a tree hiding a fawn.

A hairy, round giant who counted his loot

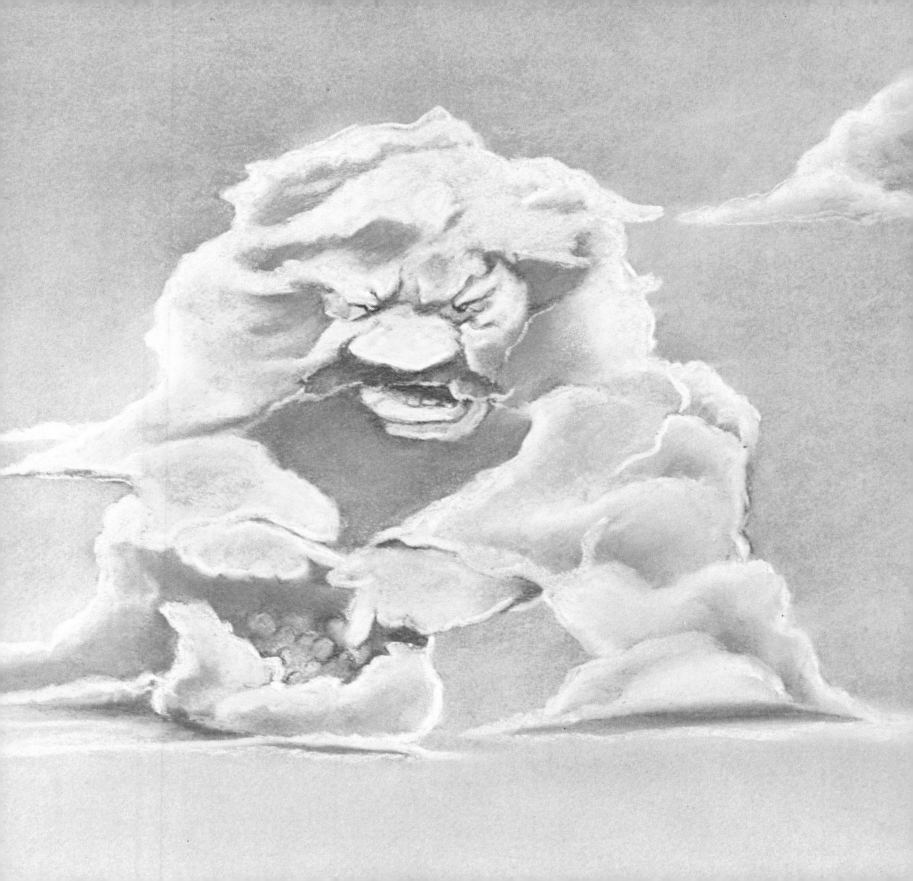

changed into a fat bear removing his boot.

Across the green field in a far away place

were terrible, huge monsters running a race.

A small, hungry gray mouse nibbling cheese

looked now like three crows on an elephant's knees.

A turtle, a rabbit, a rat, and raccoon

were tagging each other above the lagoon,

when a feathery lady riding a snail

changed into a lizard that tickled a whale.

As the sky grew all cluttered with shapes of gray
a distant rumble interrupted the play:

clouds tumbled along and flew quickly on by,
some were low and long,
some were round and quite high.

More billowing shapes came to join the parade,
the sun was all gone and the earth all in shade—

when some frightening fish playing chase with a plane

made this cumulous fun turn into soft rain.

So Laura and Brian went inside to play,
they'd watch for their friends on the next cloudy day.